W9-CKJ-084

VELOCIRAPTOR

REVISED EDITION

A TRUE BOOK®

by
Elaine Landau

Children's Press®
A Division of Scholastic Inc.

New York Toronto London Auckland Sydney
Mexico City New Delhi Hong Kong
Danbury, Connecticut

The ferocious *Velociraptor*

Content Consultant
Susan H. Gray, MS, Zoology,
Little Rock, Arkansas

Reading Consultant
Cecilia Minden-Cupp, PhD
*Former Director, Language and
Literacy Program
Harvard Graduate School of
Education*

Author's Dedication
For Allie

*The photograph on the cover
and the title page shows a
model of Velociraptor.*

Library of Congress Cataloging-in-Publication Data
Landau, Elaine.
    Velociraptor / by Elaine Landau. — Rev. ed.
        p. cm. — (A true book)
    Includes bibliographical references and index.
    ISBN-10: 0-531-16833-6 (lib. bdg.)   0-531-15473-4 (pbk.)
    ISBN-13: 978-0-531-16833-2 (lib. bdg.)   978-0-531-15473-1 (pbk.)
    1. Velociraptor—Juvenile literature. I. Title. II. Series.
QE862.S3L38 2007
567.912–dc22
                                                    2006004424

CHILDREN'S PRESS, and A TRUE BOOK™, and associated logos are
trademarks and/or registered trademarks of Scholastic Library Publishing.
SCHOLASTIC and associated logos are trademarks and/or registered
trademarks of Scholastic Inc.
1 2 3 4 5 6 7 8 9 10 R 16 15 14 13 12 11 10 09 08 07

Contents

Long ago, many kinds of dinosaurs and reptiles roamed Earth.

Long, Long Ago

Earth looked different millions of years ago. It was home to a lot of **prehistoric** creatures. Many of these creatures were huge dinosaurs. Some were more than 20 feet (6 meters) tall. A few had tails more than 18 feet (5 m) long.

There were small dinosaurs as well as large ones during a time known as the Age of the Dinosaurs. The Age of the Dinosaurs lasted from 250 million years ago to about 65 million years ago. What these smaller dinosaurs lacked in size, they made up for in other ways.

One small but deadly dinosaur was called *Velociraptor*. It lived about 70 million years ago. *Velociraptor* was about 3 feet (1 m) tall and 5 to 6 feet (1.5 m) long.

Smaller dinosaurs like these lived among larger dinosaurs.

It weighed 15 to 30 pounds (7 to 14 kilograms). Today, many dogs weigh more than that.

Velociraptor was a **ferocious**

meat eater. It often killed **prey** several times larger than itself. To find out more about this dinosaur, keep reading.

Velociraptor was a small dinosaur, but a skilled hunter.

Meet the Speedy Thief

Velociraptor was a small but powerful **theropod**, or meat eater. The name *Velociraptor* means "speedy thief." These creatures were fast on their feet. They could run as fast

The name *Velociraptor* means "speedy thief," because this dinosaur was quick on its feet.

as 40 miles (64 kilometers) per hour for a short time.

Velociraptor could easily outrun the larger, plant-eating dinosaurs it hunted. The plant eaters, such as *Triceratops*, were slowed down by their huge size. *Velociraptor* didn't weigh nearly as much as the plant eaters. Because it had hollow bones, *Velociraptor* was lighter and faster.

Like many meat-eating dinosaurs, *Velociraptor* held its tail up stiffly when moving. Its stiff tail did more than help the dinosaur keep its balance. *Velociraptor* could change direction quickly by swinging its tail. The animal rarely had

Velociraptor's long tail helped the dinosaur to change direction quickly.

to slow down, which made it an effective **predator**.

   Velociraptor has been described as a living weapon. It had a long, narrow skull armed with strong, well-developed jaw muscles. One set of muscles allowed the dinosaur to open its jaws wide. Other muscles let its jaws snap shut tightly on its prey. A third muscle group made *Velociraptor*'s bite forceful enough to tear flesh easily.

This *Velociraptor* fossil shows the dinosaur's narrow skull and strong jaws for catching and holding prey.

Velociraptor's teeth curved inward, which made it difficult for prey to escape.

Velociraptor's jaws were lined with rows of sharp, jagged teeth. Its teeth curved inward to hold its prey more tightly in its mouth. This stopped the dinosaur's victim from escaping.

Velociraptor also had long, strong arms and hands. Each hand had three fingers with sharply pointed claws. These claws helped the small dinosaur hold on to its prey.

Velociraptor's feet were designed for more than fast movement. Its feet were ideal for attacking victims. Each foot had four toes with long claws. However, the second toe of each foot had an especially large, hooked claw.

The Perfect Predator

Velociraptor had still other features that made it a prehistoric killing machine. These creatures had excellent hearing and eyesight, along with a good sense of smell. They were probably able to hear and smell prey from a distance. Having keen vision helped this dinosaur to spot prey quickly and chase it down.

Velociraptor had keen senses, which made it an effective predator.

Velociraptor's front and back claws were powerful weapons.

Paleontologists—scientists who study prehistoric life— have often debated about how *Velociraptor* used its long claws. Paleontologists used to believe these claws were powerful slicing tools.

They thought that *Velociraptor* might have used them to rip open its prey.

To test this idea, scientists designed a mechanical claw like *Velociraptor's*. The mechanical claw was attached to a robot arm and tested on a large piece of pork belly. Pork belly—the part of a hog from which bacon comes—is similar to a dinosaur's **hide**.

The results were surprising. *Velociraptor's* claws weren't

strong enough to rip open flesh. *Velociraptor* probably pounced on its prey and gripped it with its claws. Then the hungry dinosaur would

A pack of *Velociraptor* could easily attack and kill much larger prey.

have used its powerful teeth and jaws to kill the prey.

Velociraptor was believed to be among the more intelligent dinosaurs. Its brain was fairly large for an animal its size. Some paleontologists believe *Velociraptor* was a smart dinosaur.

These small, swift hunters worked well together. Paleontologists believe *Velociraptor* probably hunted in groups called packs.

First, several *Velociraptor* might strike at a plant eater's tail. Others would bite and tear at its hind, or rear, legs.

It is likely that the final and most deadly blows came from a third group of *Velociraptor*. They would spring into action once the plant eater had stopped running. Using their teeth and jaws, they would bite and tear apart their victim. This is how small *Velociraptor* was able to hunt down much larger dinosaurs.

Fossil Finds

Paleontologists learn about dinosaurs by studying **fossils**. Fossils are evidence of plants and animals that lived long ago. Fossils might include bones, footprints, teeth, or leaf imprints on rocks. Over time, some of these remains turn to rock.

Dinosaur hunters have learned about different dinosaurs by piecing the fossils together. It is like putting the pieces of a jigsaw puzzle together.

One of the world's greatest fossil finds took place in Mongolia in 1971. Here the skeletons of *Velociraptor* and another dinosaur were locked together. *Velociraptor* had used its right arm to grasp the head of the plant-eating

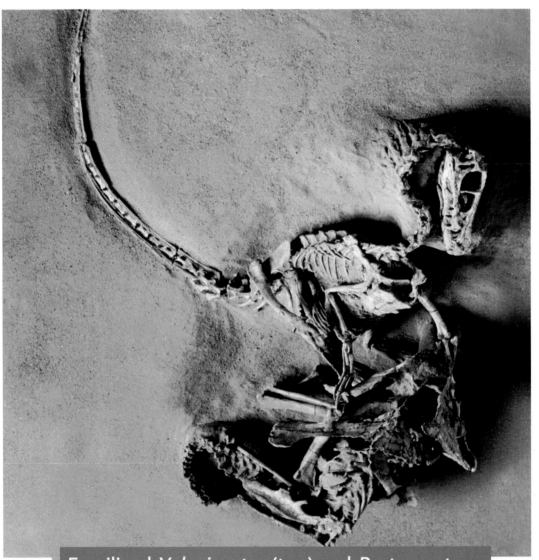

Fossilized *Velociraptor* (top) and *Protoceratops* (bottom) were killed while fighting.

horned dinosaur called *Proto-ceratops*. But the horned dinosaur fought hard to defend itself. It used its jaws to break *Velociraptor*'s right arm.

Both dinosaurs died in the battle. Paleontologists think that a collapsing sand dune may have buried them alive. The skeletons of these fighting dinosaurs were buried in the desert for millions of years. In 1971, a team of Polish and Mongolian scientists found them.

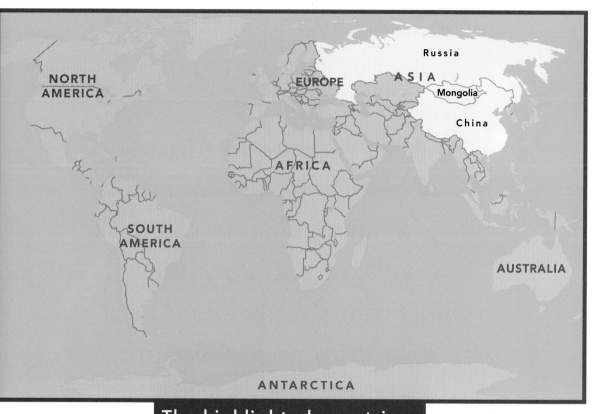

NORTH
AMERICA

EUROPE

ASIA

Russia

Mongolia

China

AFRICA

SOUTH
AMERICA

AUSTRALIA

ANTARCTICA

The highlighted countries on this map are where *Velociraptor* fossils have been found.

The fossils from the dinosaurs' deadly battle are a national treasure of Mongolia.

Other *Velociraptor* fossils have been found in Mongolia, Russia, and China. In Mongolia, the skulls of two very young *Velociraptor* were found near an *Oviraptor* nest. *Oviraptor* was a small, fast-moving, bird-like dinosaur.

The skulls may have been the remains of a meal. Very young *Velociraptor* often did

This desert in Mongolia has been the site of important *Velociraptor* discoveries.

not live long. They were easy prey for *Oviraptor* to provide food for its young. But *Velociraptor* that survived grew into skilled hunters.

All in the Family

Velociraptor belonged to a family of meat-eating dinosaurs known as **dromaeosaurids**. The name means "running lizards." All these dinosaurs leaped on their prey when attacking.

Most dromaeosaurids were small. For a long time, the

largest was thought to be only between 10 and 11 feet (about 3 m) long. However, more recently, *Utahraptor* was discovered. Its name means "Utah thief." It was found in Utah. This relative of *Velociraptor* measured more than 19 feet (almost 6 m) long.

There have been some other interesting dromaeosaurid family finds. A team of Chinese and American scientists found a fossil

A relative of *Velociraptor* was covered in feathers.

skeleton of a dinosaur related to *Velociraptor* in northeastern China. Paleontologists studied the skeleton. They found that when the dinosaur was alive, its body was covered in soft feathers.

The discovery excited paleontologists. It was more proof that modern birds are related to meat-eating dinosaurs. Birds and dinosaurs have more than one hundred things in common. Paleontologists now think that dromaeosaurids, like *Velociraptor*, are most closely related to birds. According to paleontologist Mark Norell, dinosaurs such as *Velociraptor* "may have looked more like weird birds than giant lizards."

Finding New Relatives

Still another discovery showed that *Velociraptor* had a really interesting relative called *Buitreraptor*. *Buitreraptor* is a dinosaur that looked like a bird. It was about the size of a large rooster. This 90-million-year-old dinosaur was found in Argentina. It is believed to be the earliest member of the dromaeosaurid family. *Velociraptor* also belonged to this family.

Paleontologists believe dromaeosaurids lived on Earth for a very long time. They also believe dromaeosaurids may have lived all over the world.

A *Buitreraptor* skeleton

Paleontologists wonder if dromaeo-saurids may have developed differently in different places. *Buitreraptor* had a long, slender snout and small, widely spaced teeth. Its teeth didn't have the jagged edges found in *Velociraptor* and other relatives from Asia and North America.

The Age of the Dinosaurs lasted for about 180 million years.

The Dinosaur Disappearance

The Age of the Dinosaurs lasted about 180 million years. During this age, different kinds of dinosaurs lived and then died out. No kind of dinosaur survived for the entire time. Most kinds of dinosaurs existed for only a few million years.

Fossils show that *Veloc-iraptor* probably died out about 70 million years ago. Some of its relatives lived later. About 65 million years ago, however, all the dino-saurs remaining on Earth

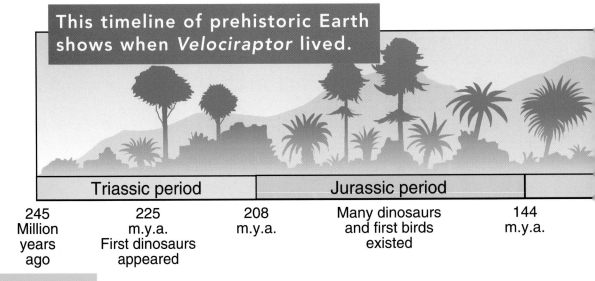

This timeline of prehistoric Earth shows when *Velociraptor* lived.

Triassic period		Jurassic period	
245 Million years ago	225 m.y.a. First dinosaurs appeared	208 m.y.a.	Many dinosaurs and first birds existed	144 m.y.a.

died. This did not happen suddenly, but over a period of about a million years.

Paleontologists are not sure why various dinosaurs died out when they did. During the Age of the Dinosaurs, Earth was

(Note:"m.y.a." means "million years ago")

| Cretaceous period | Tertiary period | |

| 80-70 m.y.a. Velociraptor existed | 65 m.y.a. Last dinosaurs became extinct | 1.6 m.y.a. First humans appeared |

still changing. The large land-masses called continents had not finished forming. Seas and mountain ranges were still taking shape. Different kinds of plant life appeared. It is likely that dinosaurs couldn't survive all these changes.

Many paleontologists think the dinosaurs died out after an asteroid crashed into Earth. Asteroids are large, rocky, planetlike bodies that move through space. If an

Paleontologists believe an asteroid like this one crashed into Earth.

asteroid struck Earth, a huge crater, or hole, would have been created.

The dust from the hole would have floated up into the **atmosphere** to form thick, dark clouds. These clouds would have blocked out the sun. Earth would have become very cold. The dinosaurs probably could not have survived the cold temperatures.

The dinosaurs will never return. We have only their fossils. From those fossils, we can continue to learn about dinosaurs like small, fierce *Velociraptor*.

We may learn even more about *Velociraptor* once this fossil is removed from the sand.

To Find Out More

Here are some additional resources to help you learn more about *Velociraptor*:

 **Books**

Foran, Jill. **Dinosaurs**. Weigl Publishers, 2004.

Susan H. Gray. **Velociraptor**. Child's World, 2004.

Jenkins, Steve. **Prehistoric Actual Size**. Houghton Mifflin, 2005.

Larson, Peter L. and Kristin Donnan. **Bones Rock! Everything You Need to Know to Become a Paleontologist**. Invisible Cities Press, 2004.

Schomp, Virginia. **Velociraptor and the Small Speedy Meat-Eaters**. Benchmark Books, 2003.

Organizations and Online Sites

Dinosaur Dig—San Diego Natural History Museum
http://www.sdnhm.org/kids/ fossils

Visit this Web site to learn about where and how to find fossils.

Journey Through Time
http://www.nhm.org/journey

Read all about different dinosaurs—including meat eaters like *Velociraptor*.

Project Exploration
950 East 61st Street
Chicago, IL 60637
http://www.info@projectex- ploration.org

This organization works to increase students' interest in paleontology.

Important Words

atmosphere the blanket of gases that surrounds Earth

dromaeosaurid the dinosaur family to which *Velociraptor* belongs

ferocious fierce

fossils evidence of plants and animals that lived long ago. Fossils might include bones, footprints, teeth, or leaf imprints on rocks.

hide an animal's skin

predator an animal that hunts other animals for food

prehistoric from the time before history was recorded

prey an animal that is hunted by another animal for food

theropod meat eater

Index

Meet the Author

Award-winning author Elaine Landau worked as a newspaper reporter, an editor, and a youth-services librarian before becoming a full-time writer. She has written more than 250 nonfiction books for young people, including True Books on animals, countries, and food. Ms. Landau has a bachelor's degree in English and journalism from New York University as well as a master's degree in library and information science. She lives with her husband and son in Miami, Florida.